© Copyright 2021 - All rights reserved.

You may not reproduce, duplicate or send the contents of this book without direct written permission from the author. You cannot hereby despite any circumstance blame the publisher or hold him or her to legal responsibility for any reparation, compensations, or monetary forfeiture owing to the information included herein, either in a direct or an indirect way.

Legal Notice: This book has copyright protection. You can use the book for personal purpose. You should not sell, use, alter, distribute, quote, take excerpts or paraphrase in part or whole the material contained in this book without obtaining the permission of the author first.

Disclaimer Notice: You must take note that the information in this document is for casual reading and entertainment purposes only. We have made every attempt to provide accurate, up to date and reliable information. We do not express or imply guarantees of any kind. The persons who read admit that the writer is not occupied in giving legal, financial, medical or other advice. We put this book content by sourcing various places.

Please consult a licensed professional before you try any techniques shown in this book. By going through this document, the book lover comes to an agreement that under no situation is the author accountable for any forfeiture, direct or indirect, which they may incur because of the use of material contained in this document, including, but not limited to, — errors, omissions, or inaccuracies.

This coloring book belongs to ....

`At the touch of love everyone becomes a poet.`
Plato

George Sand
`There is only one happiness in this life, to love and be loved.`

Leo Christopher
`I swear I couldn't love you more than I do right now, and yet I know I will tomorrow.`

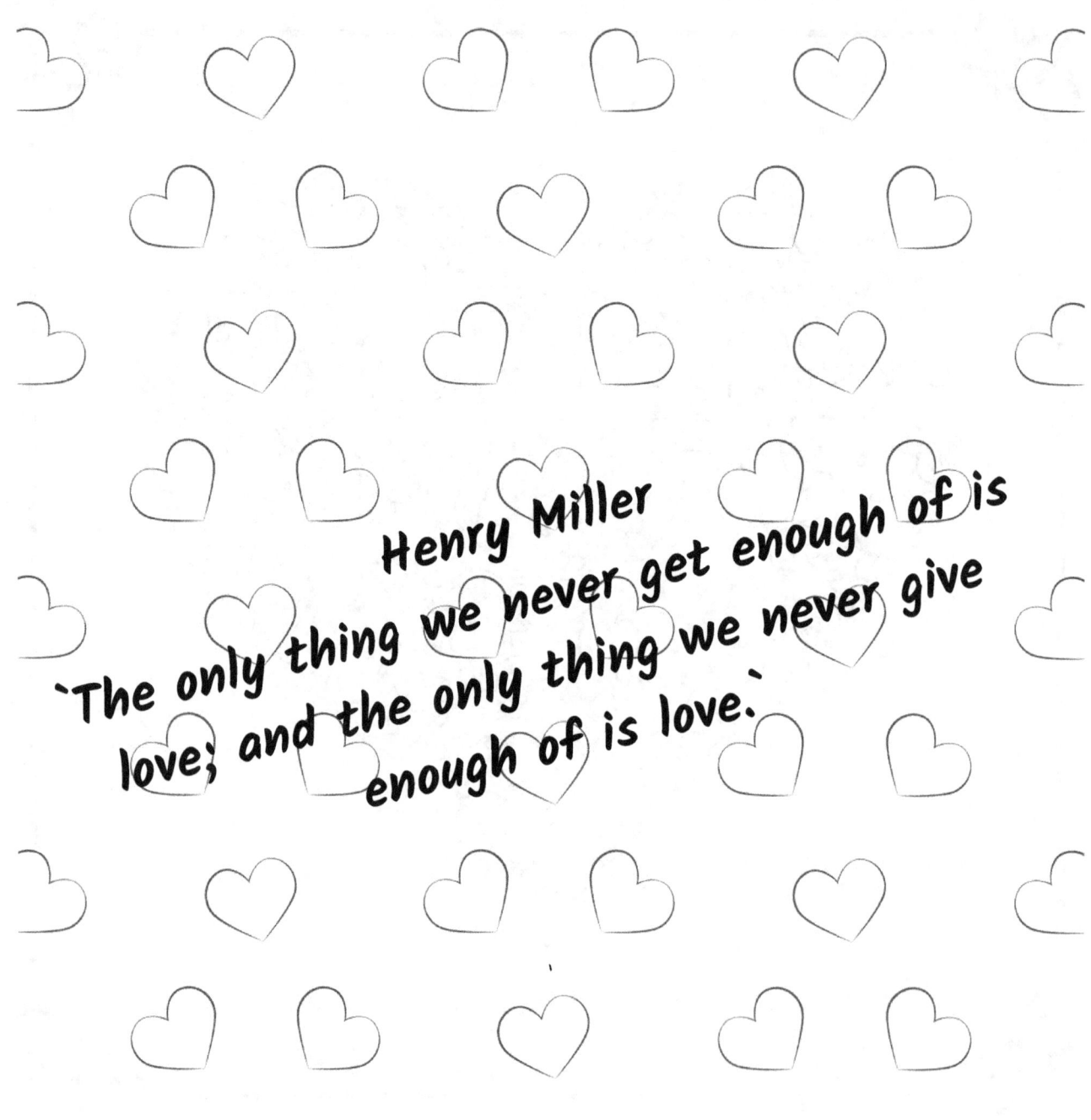

Henry Miller

`The only thing we never get enough of is love; and the only thing we never give enough of is love.`

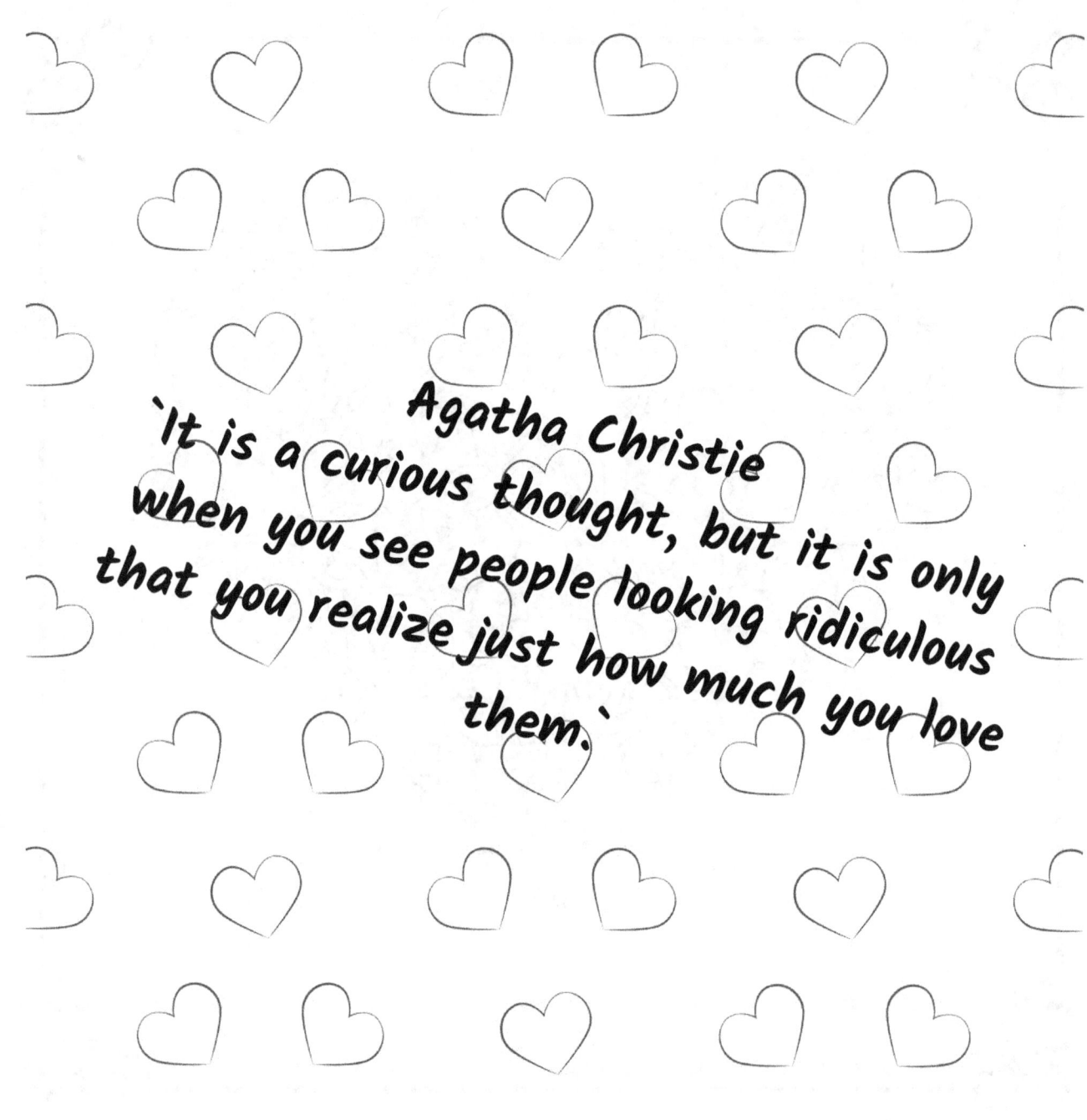

Agatha Christie
`It is a curious thought, but it is only when you see people looking ridiculous that you realize just how much you love them.`

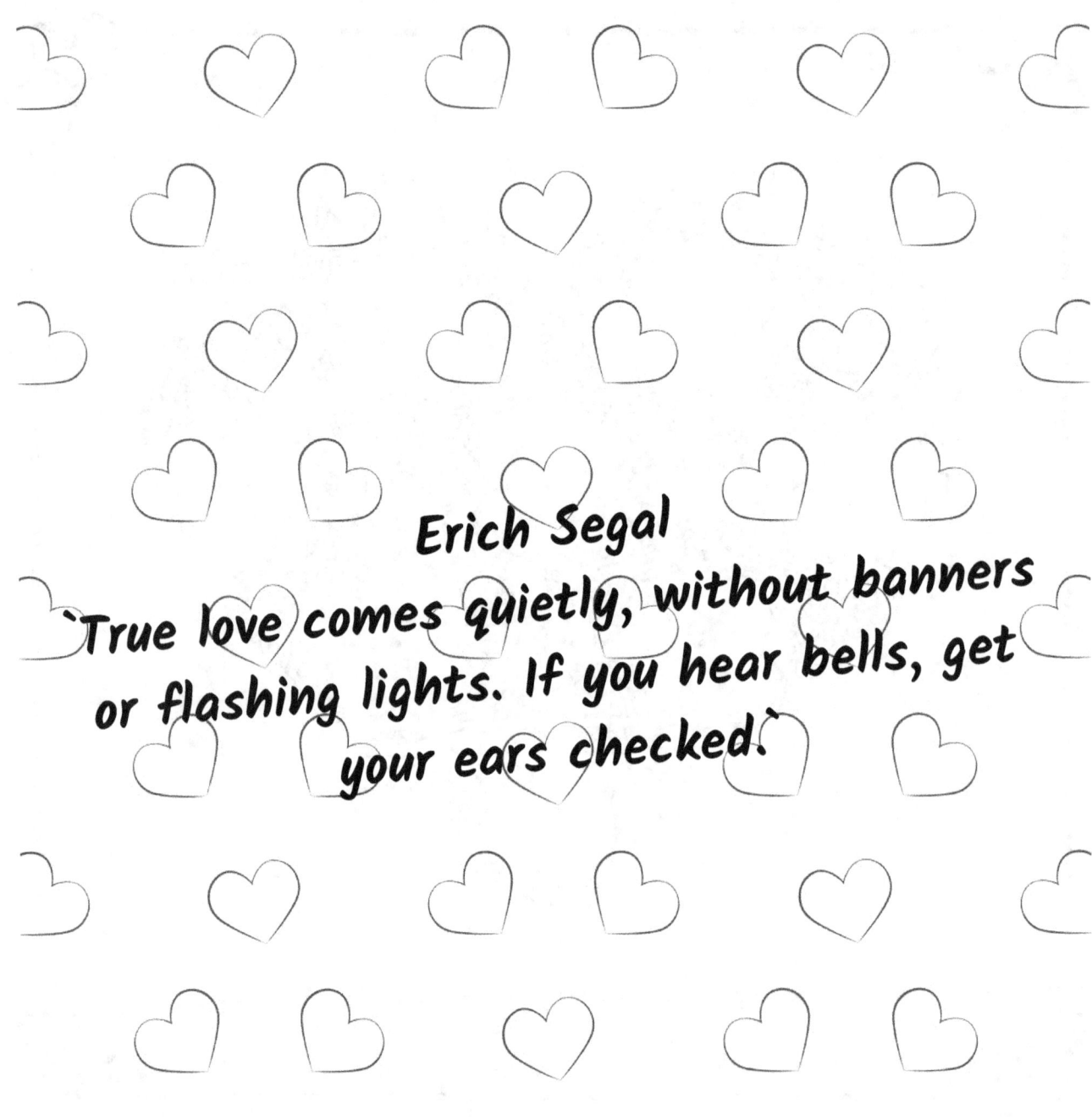

Erich Segal

`True love comes quietly, without banners or flashing lights. If you hear bells, get your ears checked.`

David Viscott
`To love and be loved is to feel the sun from both sides.`

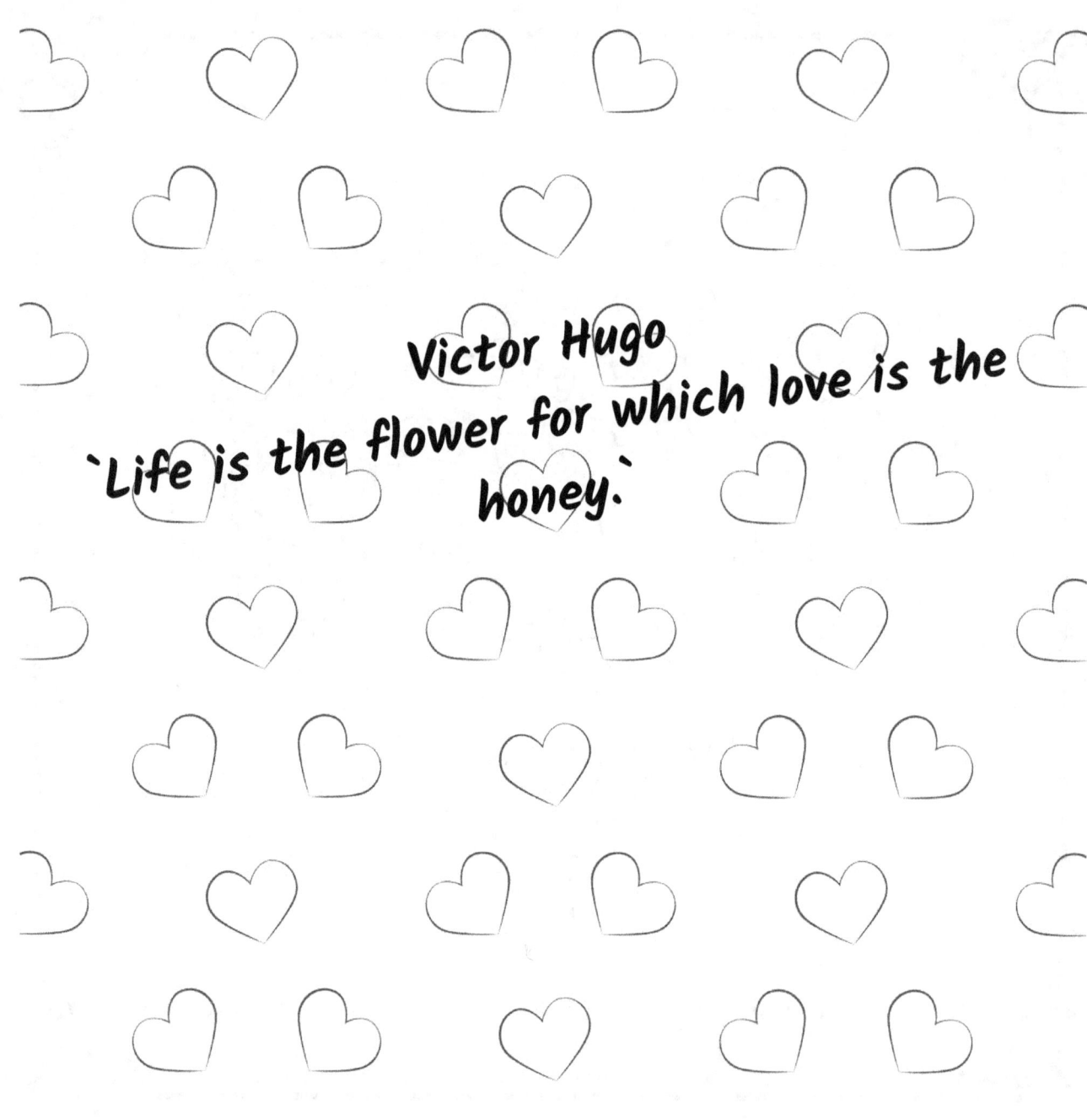

Lao Tzu
`Being deeply loved by someone gives you strength, while loving someone deeply gives you courage.`

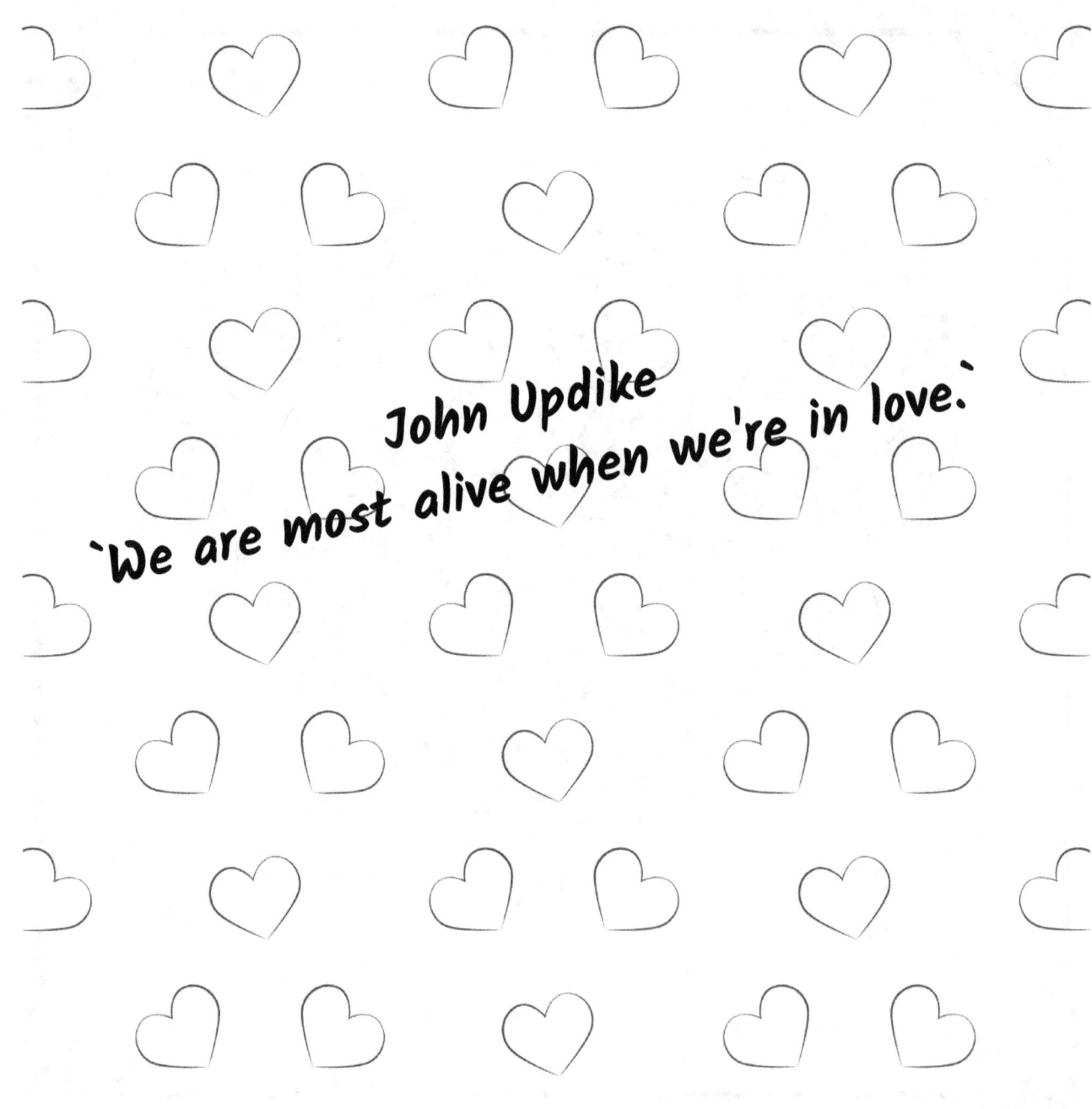

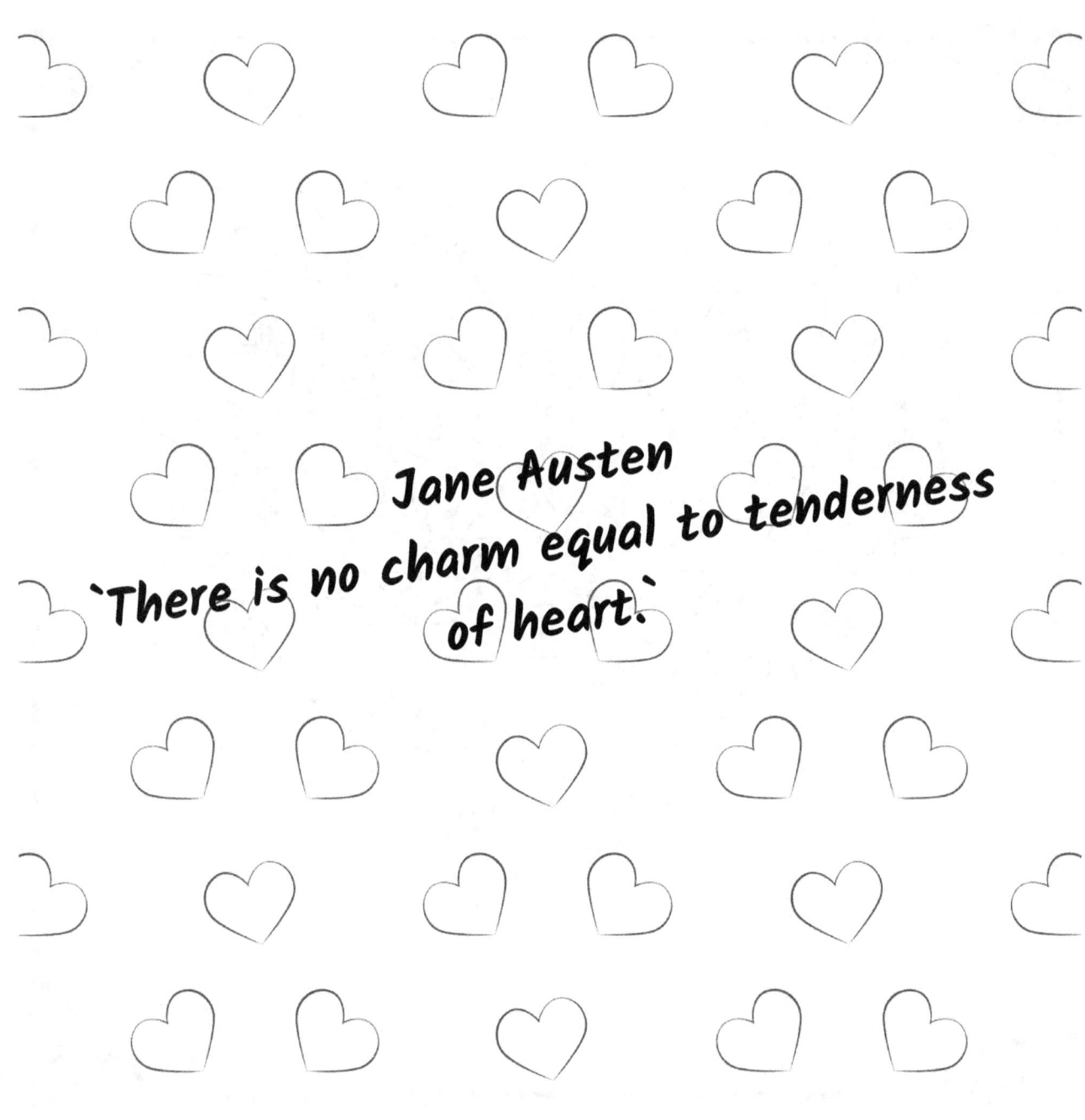

Blaise Pascal
`The heart has its reasons of which reason knows nothing.`

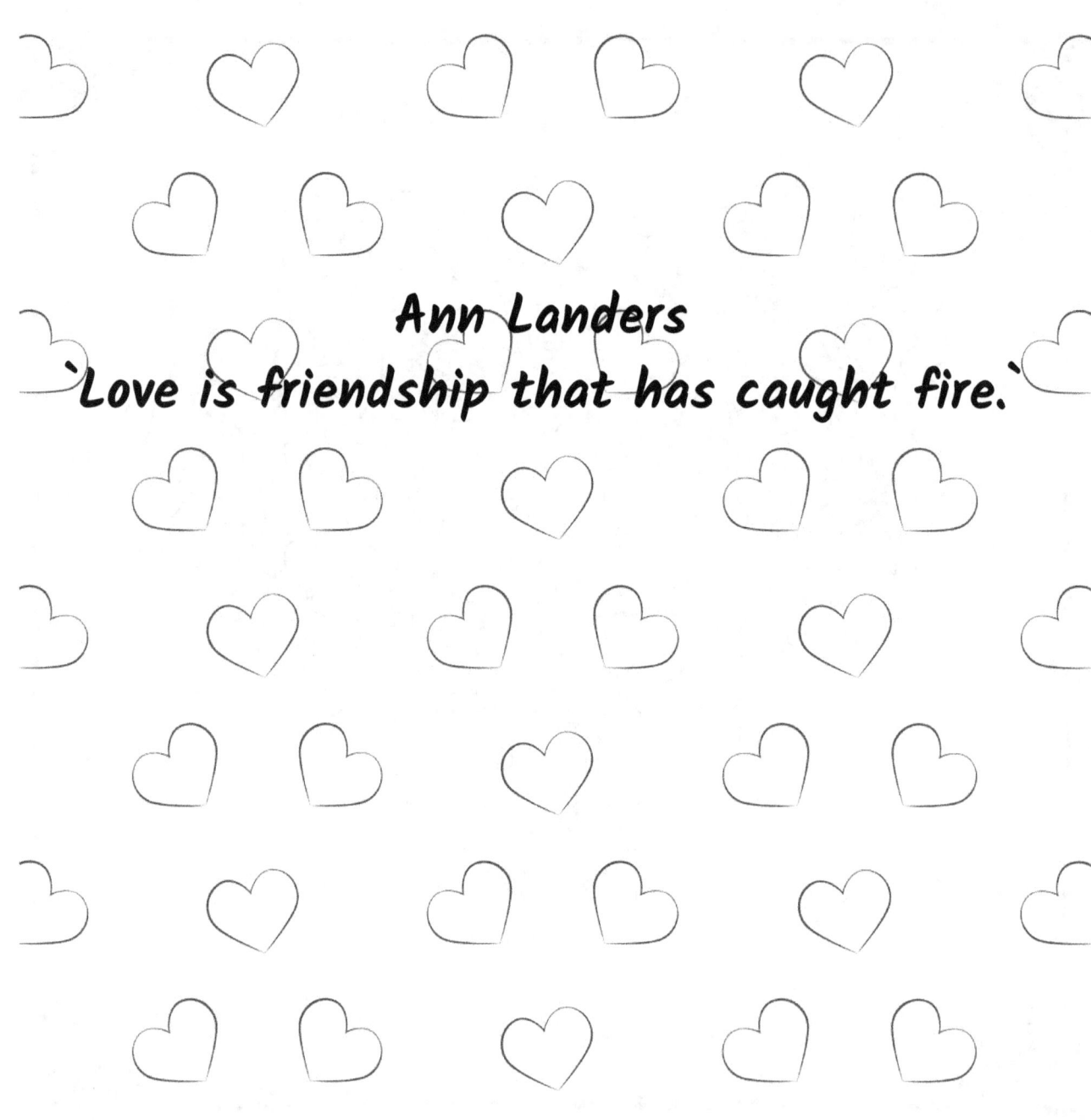

Ann Landers
`Love is friendship that has caught fire.`

Lucille Ball
`Love yourself first and everything falls into line.`

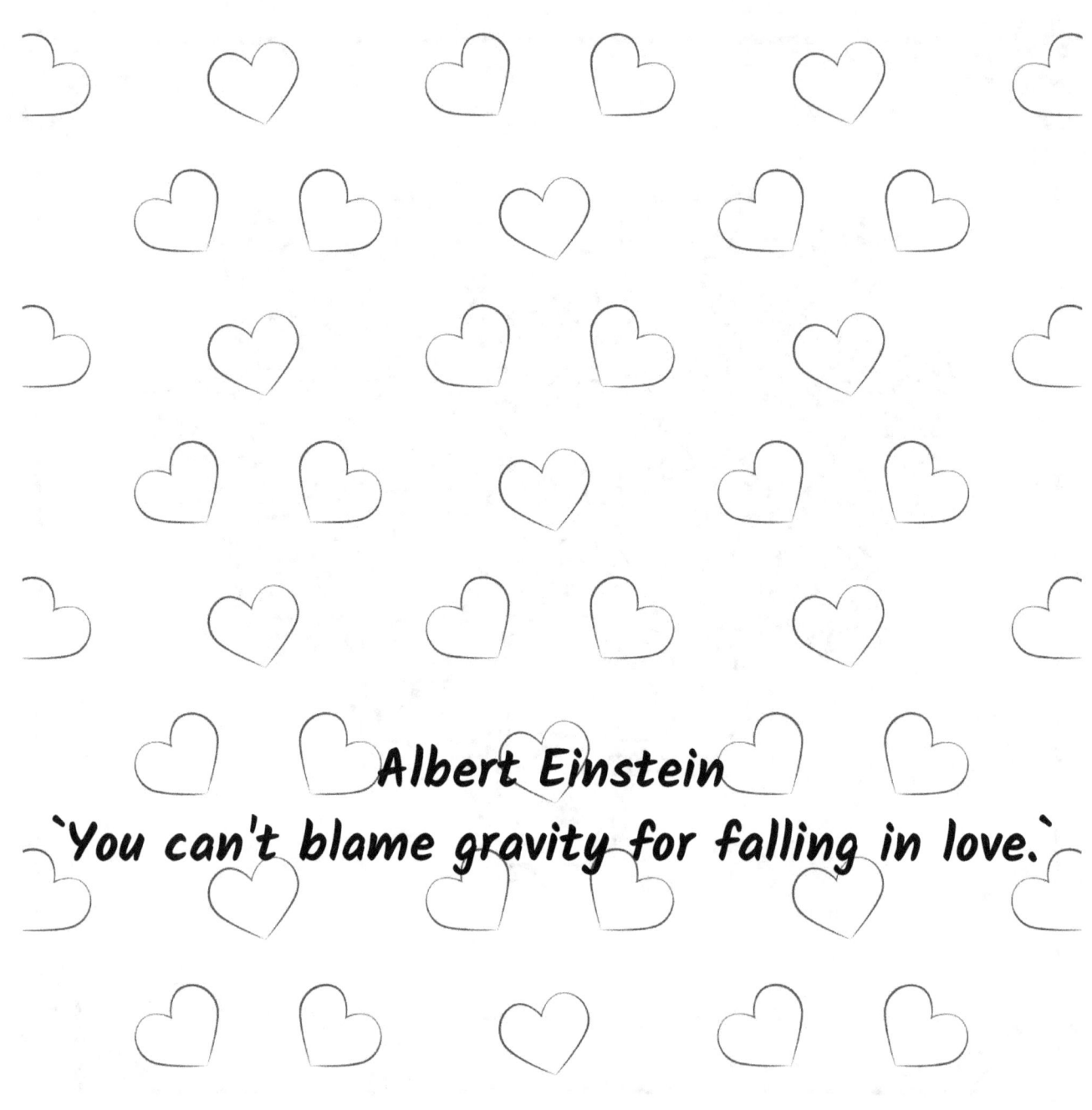

Albert Einstein
`You can't blame gravity for falling in love.`

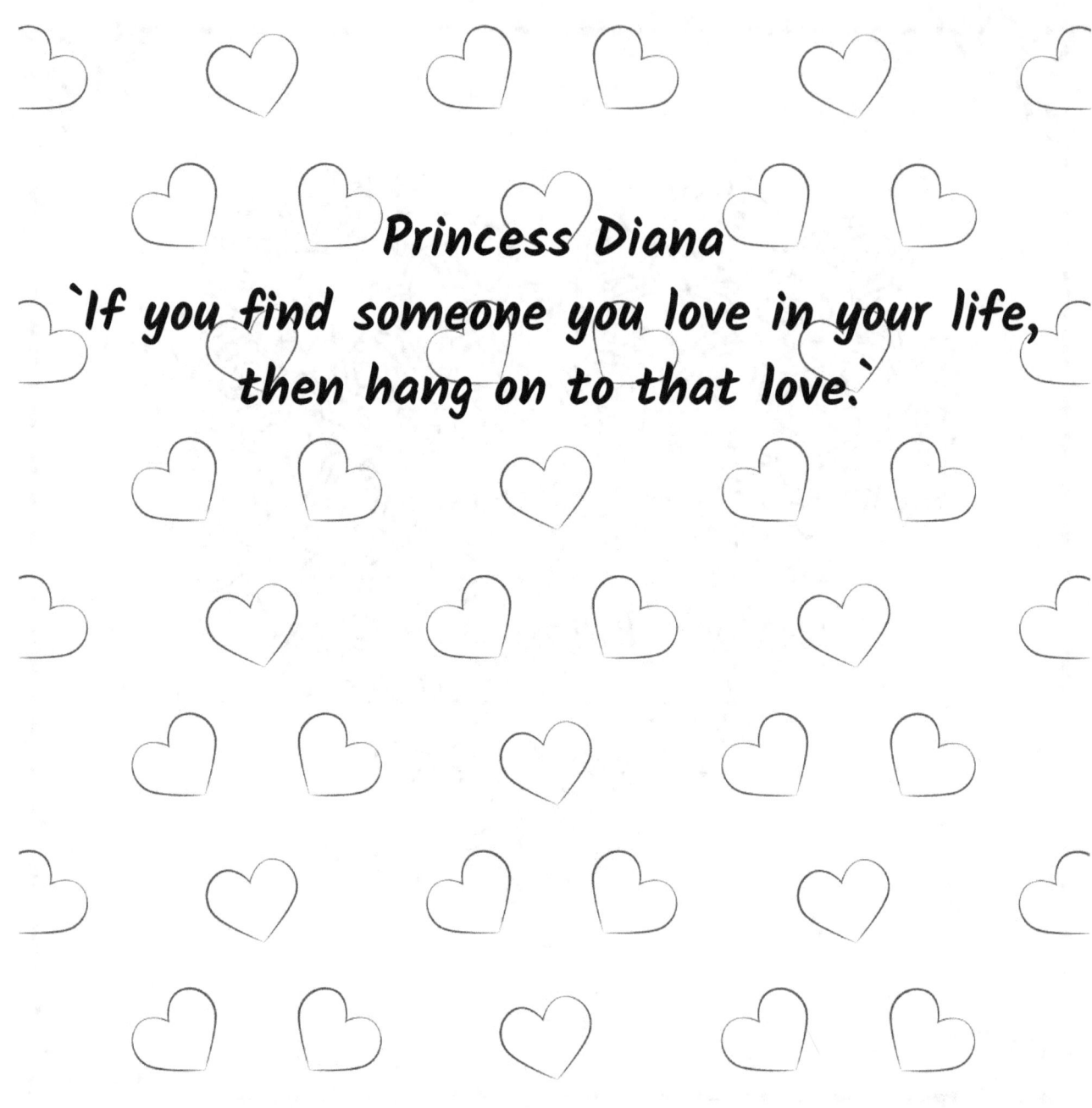

Princess Diana
`If you find someone you love in your life, then hang on to that love.`

Frank Sinatra
`A simple "I love you" means more than money.`

Richard Bach
`True love stories never have endings.`

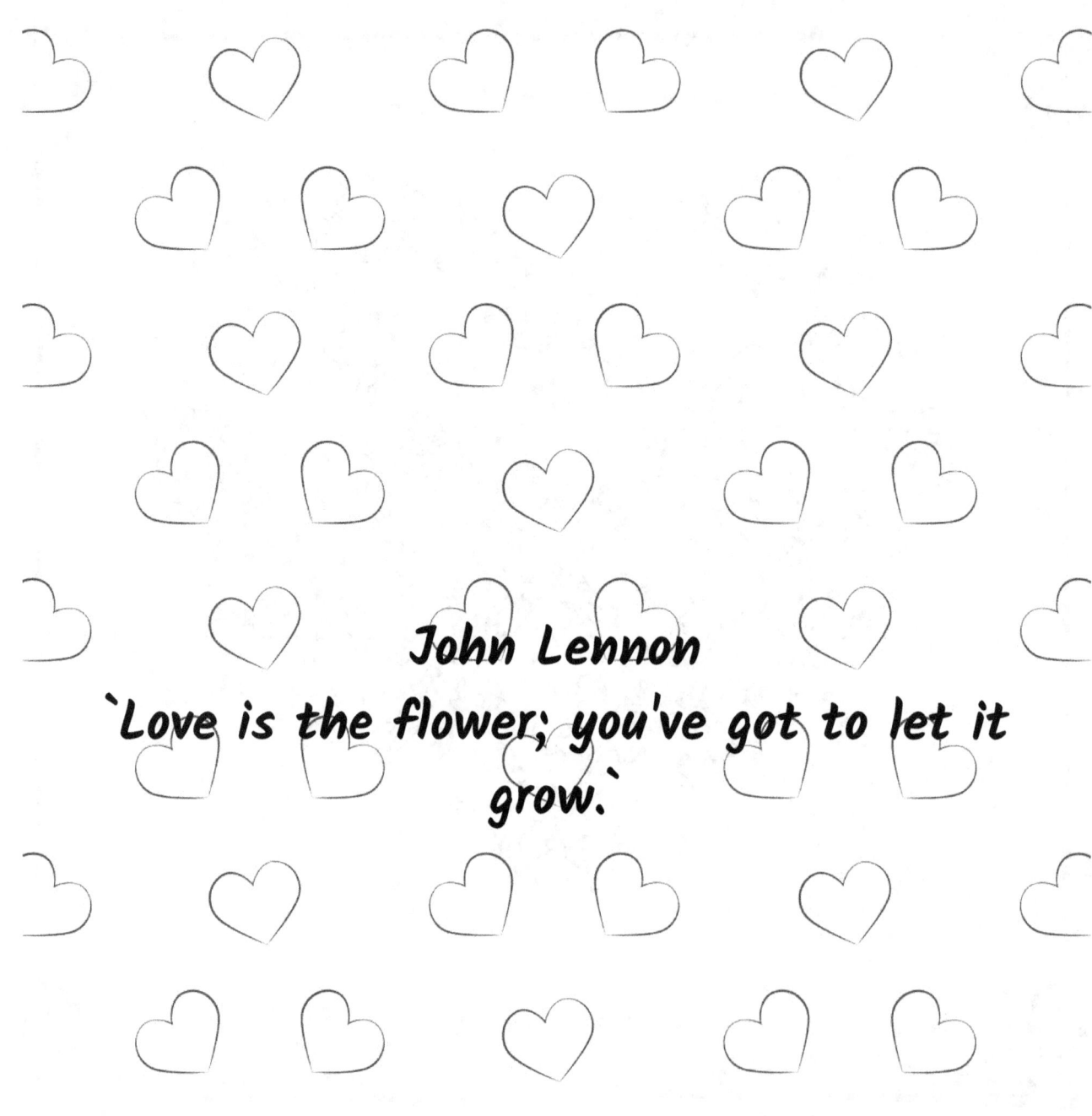

John Lennon
`Love is the flower; you've got to let it grow.`

Zelda Fitzgerald
`Nobody has ever measured, not even poets, how much the heart can hold.`

Thank you!
I hope you enjoyed this book as much as I loved making it.
Your opinion is very important to me. Please let me know how you like this coloring book at:

vlascu77@yahoo.com

www.ingramcontent.com/pod-product-compliance
Lightning Source LLC
Chambersburg PA
CBHW081312070526
44578CB00006B/848